I0191421

Every Color Of My Sky

A collection of heart warming poems

MAYANK SALUJA

/ BookLeaf
Publishing

India | USA | UK

Made with ❤ on the BookLeaf Publishing Platform
www.bookleafpub.in
www.bookleafpub.com

Dedication

Ever imagine life without thoughts. The thoughts that develop in our sub conscious mind make us travel through our imagination and provide eternal peace. This is what writing does to you. This is what writing does to me. I have never imagined myself to be a writer at any point in my life. But when I started developing the habit of writing, it gradually started to intrigue me.

I use to read books, different thoughts penned down by various writers in the world and I used to travel into the world that they describe in their writing. This is what writing does to me. I gradually started to have interest in writing and slowly I started to enjoy it with extreme passion.

Today is the day, as I m sharing with you the thoughts of my mind that either made me awake whole night or just kept coming in my mind from time to time, but I thought of sharing it with you the way I have started to develop interest in writing and what my mind goes into.

I thought of writing a book sometimes back but never thought I would be able to complete it, but today as you all would be holding the dream I had once saw, it is likely to be fulfilled now. This is not just a book, it's my life until now what I have seen through my eyes and what people have shown me through their perspective.

I believe that once you hold this book in your hand, you will imagine how happy my face will be for accepting my work to which I gave my full heart and soul, and once you go through the pages, you may relate to each and every thought that I put into this book.

I wish you all will have the same smile as I had when you chose to pick my book. I can guarantee you that you won't be disappointed once you read this by your heart. A dream is what you are holding in your hand; a success is what you will be having after reading this book on your face.

Happy reading to my readers and thank you for accepting me!!

Preface

This book is going to get birth because of the extensive efforts and dedication that has been put behind each words.

Writing is something that gives me immense satisfaction and peace when i am lost in the world of words and dreams. It is my way of learning to listen to myself, to silence and to the stories hidden in everyday life. These poems will transform you and make you belief in the stories that are being created in the world around us.

Acknowledgements

To begin with, I would like to thank the almighty for making me achieve my goal of writing something which can belong to the world.

I coud not start without thanking my parents for always believing in me, my sister, brother in law and my little munchkins my nephews for always stand by me during each time i have struggled. To my wife, whose love and constant motivation drove me to write what i have brought to you through this book.

This journey would not be possible without my friends who have always encouraged me to write and alwasy have been waiting for me to bring out the best.

Abhishek, Jahnvi, Manish, Prasanjeet my all time motivational family of friends.

Mohit, Sudhanshu, Nikhil, Nimit, Akshay, Tarun for always been constant critics and for your honest opinion on my writing.

Aishwarya my long distance friend, who have supported and encouraged me everytiime i have tried to gave up.

To all the friends i have made through this journey, if I am not able to speak your name then i am sorry but remember you are always there in my thoughts.

Last but not the least to all of you readers, for trusting me, believing in me and for holding this book and

making my dream come true through your support.
Thank You All!! Love you!!

Happy Reading :)

1. Life is that song

Life is that song,
To the melody it belong,
Soothing the ears with it's chime,
Like a bird playing and dancing to its rhyme
This is our life, to us it belong
We are to stay here no matter for how long,
Let's make our life worth living for,
Forgetting how it has been before,
New life is waiting for us ahead,
Let's go and make it best of the best.

2. Terror of the Past

In the darkness of terror,
That i faced in the past,
Somehow they are,
Running in so fast,
No where to go,
I feel so caged,
One day I will be free from it,
I will no longer be afraid.

3. Far away from here

There is a world, where there is no fear,
It's not near, but far away from here,
Where love blossoms between two hearts,
Where bonds are thick and no one to apart,
Where people can share what they feel,
Where people takes no time to heal,
Where life is good, no stress is there,
Everything seems bright and crystal clear.

4. The night, stars and us

When the night is dark,
And the thunder spark,
You walk into my dream,
Where i would scream,
Your name again and again,
In the unstoppable rain,
Entangled with love in our eyes,
We make the night memorable for life...

5. Dream of me and you

I dream of a world with me and you,
No one in my life is better than you,
You are so constant in my life,
I dream of us as man and wife,

Your eyes talk to me,
As the world stands still,
My once empty heart,
Now with love it is filled,

My heart craves for you everyday,
Think about you night and day,
I wish there is some other way,
So that you are here with me to stay,

I wish to hold you tight,
For you I could put up any fight,
To make you feel special all right,
With you there's nothing wrong & everything right

I love you now, i love you forever,
I promise you, i'll forget you never,
You made my life shining bright,
For you, I wanna do everything right

I wish you achieve all that you desire,
Make each and everyone to get inspire,
I know you will overcome all the obstacles in life,
I promise I'll be there to witness through my eyes,

All the best for everything you do,
Keep everyone happy and yourself too,
I love you and I'll be there with you,
Till death apart, I'll be sticking to you..

6. Life and Moment

Life is about enjoying,
Every moment with joy,
It is not a game to play,
It is not a toy,
Fill it with happy moments
For it may not come again,
Life is to cherish moments,
Without any kind of pain,
May this life brings you,
Everything that you desire,
Fulfill every dream of yours
That you truly aspire.

7. Self Esteem

I might never,
See you again,
I will have to,
Carry that pain,
I'll never forget the time,
All that went in vain,
Now i ask for,
A little rain,
So that I can hide,
My tears and pain,
I will now,
Be strong again,
It's time for me,
To regain... My self esteem

8. The Sweetest Gift

When i saw your face,
I found an angel's trace,
Your charming face is all i see,
You make me go weak on my knee,
I have got you from the lord above,
The sweetest gift as pure as dove,
I'll always cherish this smile throughout,
You are a princess without a doubt.

9. Sunday

It's the weekend that comes our way,
One of the day of it is sunday,
It keeps us busy with different things,
Some household chores some other things,

The happiness follows the face when it comes,
The hectic schedule of the week gets numb,
The freshness the sunday carries with it,
Makes our worries vanish,

Though it has lost its charm these days,
Since everyday feels like Sundays,
Sitting at home working and playing,
This lockdown has made lazy mornings,

This lockdown will surely get down soon,
Sunday will feel like itself soon,
Everything will be as normal as it was before,
Lets enjoy the sunday and cherish it more..

10. The Stillness Within

After all this while, the craze has dim,
The sky has fallen, the lights got dim,
People are captured in the house,
Feels like being trapped in cage like a mouse,

Nowhere to go, nowhere to be seen,
All this long, I am looking at my screen,
The shows are getting bord, muscles getting tight,
All I need is a fresh air and a little bit of sunlight,

Don't know when all this will come to an end,
The time of our life is just getting bend,
I wish someone stop all this fuzz,
So that we can have a little bit of buzz...

11. The untold feeling

The love that shines in your eyes,
Is so true and pure,
I wish that love was mine,
So warm and so pure,
It's your love that would have made me happy,
It's your love I urge for more,
But you have given your heart to someone
Whom you loved & and i couldn't ask for more...

12. Story

Everyone has a story to tell,
They may know, they may don't know,
Every story has a spell,
You might never know,

Each story has a beauty,
That is of it's own,
Each story may have a meaning,
In it all alone,

All stories have memories,
Sometimes good, somtimes bad,
These stories contain feelings,
Some happy, some maybe sad,

But all these stories are written,
Directly from the heart,
Let's make some more of them,
So that they are remembered till last...

13. When Summer Lost Its Charm

The summer feels incomplete,
Time is running at its speed,
Nowhere to go, don't know what to do,
Is there anything that we could do?

The season is losing it's charm,
The days are getting really warm,
No mangoes could be seen this season,
There must be some valid reason,

The house is chanting the old rhymes,
It feels like the good old times,
The bucket filled with happiness,
Helping in reducing some stress,

This too shall pass, we should pray,
Soon we will be getting back good old days,
Everything will feel alright,
Days will be again sunny and bright...

14. Love You

My love is you, my love is for few,
No one in my life is better than you,
You made me smile, you made me cry,
What in my life, I always try,
Love is a great feeling,
Love is like a play,
Love is what i feel for you,
Each and everyday..

15. Eyes

Eyes are beautiful, Eyes are sweet,
Eyes can speak when hearts meet,
Soul can speak through our eyes,
These eyes makes possible
Love at first sight,
One can see in one'e eyes,
The expression of love, hate and delight,
These thinking eyes secretly tells,
THE STORY OF LIFE...

16. Letters I wrote to you

I threw away the letters I wrote to you,
Because I know they will never reach you,
If they reach, they will never be read,
So I thought I will not send it instead,
I read them again and again for my sake,
I thought once you will understand your mistake,
The time I had with you still fresh in my mind,
You have always been so lovely and kind,
I couldn't fell out of love with you,
So i threw the letters I wrote to you,
Because I knew they will never reach you.

17. The Fire Within

Travelling on the roads of new hopes,
With new life and new scopes,
With the determination of keeping alive,
My desires to achieve my goals,

I'll work hard and give my best,
To keep myself above the rest,
I just have to work hard,
And put myself on guard,

I've to do everything right,
To make my future shine bright,
With all the blessings from Lord above,
I want to make my parents proud and loved.

18. Timeless Friendshp

Last time I met my friends,
It felt like time will never end,
We laugh, we cry, all the memories we enjoyed,
All this while those memories left a void,

The day was blossoming when we meet,
Felt like it was another birthday treat,
The bottle opened, we all got drunk,
After all it was a bit of a luck,

Last time we met, we were distance apart,
The only thing connected was our little heart,
We missed each other, we relived the memories,
Our friendship is been like Sachin's centuries,

Now and forever this friendship will last,
Together we survive, together we'll have a blast,
Our friendship, our brotherhood will go very far,
Just as far as twinkling star...

19. Books

Books are the basket, full of jewels,
Books are our best friend, when we travel,
Books give us company, when we are alone,
Books give us knowledge like the light of dawn,
Books give us knowledge which no one can steal,
This make us to achieve the goal of our life,
If we study them with concentration and zeal,
Books are the food of **soul in brief...**

20. Memories

Memories are beautiful, memories are sweet,
Memories are there when we first meet,
Memories are in the childhood we live,
Memories are there where we believe,

Memories are there in the new born,
Memories are there in flowers and thorn,
Memories are there wherever we are,
Memories are like the shining night star.

Memories are there wherever we go,
Memories are there where we don't know,
Memories will always be with you,
Whether you take it as something new,

Memories will never leave you alone,
They are here to stay forever,
It needs your believe that they are here,
In the good,bad or amazing times that are coming near...

21. No one can stop you

You have the ability in you,
There's nothing that you can't do,
You need to boost your confidence,
Whatever may be the circumstance,

You are strong, you are worthy,
Forget your pain, forget your worry,
It is the time to rise and shine,
Always carry the positive smile,

You will achieve, you will grow,
Show them all, who made you low,
You can conquer the world if you try,
Chase your dream and touch the sky,

No one can stop you, once you know,
The right path that you need to go,
To fulfill what you and your heart desire,
Ignite in you, the flames of fire,

You will reach the great heights,
Everything will feel so right,
You will be happy, you will be glad,
That you fulfilled the dream you had

22. Importance of parents

Parents are important part,
Always present in children's heart,
Pouring love in their nurturing ways,
Forget about their happiness always,

Ready to fulfill child's wish,
Serving them delicious dish,
Gives priority to their children always,
Let's keep these parents happy always,

Forget to sleep when child is in pain,
They don't let their efforts go in vain,
May god bless these parents with things they desire,
Such are the parents who always inspire..